Lerner SPORTS

ALL-STAR SMACKDOWN

COCO GAUFF VS. SERENA WILLIAMS

WHO WOULD WIN?

YOLANDA RIDGE

Lerner Publications ◆ Minneapolis

Lerner Publications Company
An imprint of Lerner Publishing Group, Inc.
241 First Avenue North
Minneapolis, MN 55401 USA

For reading levels and more information, look up this title at www.lernerbooks.com.

Main body text set in Aptifer Sans LT Pro. Typeface provided by Linotype AG.

Editor: Angel Kidd **Photo Editor**: Angel Kidd

Library of Congress Cataloging-in-Publication Data

Names: Ridge, Yolanda, 1973– author.
Title: Coco Gauff vs. Serena Williams : who would win? / Yolanda Ridge.
Other titles: Coco Gauff versus Serena Williams
Description: Minneapolis : Lerner Publications, [2025] | Series: Lerner sports. All-star smackdown | Includes bibliographical references and index. | Audience: Ages 7–11 years | Audience: Grades 2–3 | Summary: "Coco Gauff is an up-and-coming tennis star, but does she have the skills to take on Serena Williams with her numerous titles and gold medals? Find out who serves up a win in this smackdown!"— Provided by publisher.
Identifiers: LCCN 2024010822 (print) | LCCN 2024010823 (ebook) | ISBN 9798765648223 (lib. bdg.) | ISBN 9798765661383 (pbk.) | ISBN 9798765653074 (epub)
Subjects: LCSH: Tennis players—Rating of—United States—Juvenile literature. | African American women tennis players—United States—Juvenile literature. | Gauff, Coco, 2004-—Juvenile literature. | Williams, Serena, 1981-—Juvenile literature. | Sports rivalries—United States—History—Juvenile literature.
Classification: LCC GV996.5 .R534 2025 (print) | LCC GV996.5 (ebook) | DDC 796.342092/52—dc23/eng/20240415

LC record available at https://lccn.loc.gov/2024010822
LC ebook record available at https://lccn.loc.gov/2024010823

Manufactured in the United States of America
1-1010825-53380-6/14/2024

TABLE OF CONTENTS

Coco Gauff

INTRODUCTION

POWERFUL PLAYERS

Coco Gauff played in the US Open on August 31, 2022. The 18-year-old faced Elena-Gabriela Ruse in the second round. Gauff was ahead by two games, but Ruse was hot on her heels. Gauff stepped up to serve. She threw the ball in the air and swung hard. The ball exploded off her racket.

Fast Facts

- Coco Gauff won the US Open in 2023.
- At 15, Gauff was the youngest player to ever play at Wimbledon.
- Serena Williams won 23 Grand Slam singles tournaments.
- Williams was the number one female singles player in the world for 319 weeks.

The screen behind Gauff flashed a speed of 128 miles (206 km) per hour. It was the third-fastest serve in women's US Open history. Ruse tried to return the ball, but it flew out of bounds. Gauff won the point and went on to win the match.

Serena Williams served up her fastest ball in the 2013 Australian Open when she was 32. The crowd erupted in applause as she hammered the ball over the net. When Williams saw the speed of 128.6 miles (207 km) per hour, she grinned. Then she got back to work and won the match in two sets to advance to the next round.

Serena Williams

Williams reaches for the ball during the 2013 Australian Open.

Both moments are on the top 10 list of the fastest female tennis serves. Gauff is a rising tennis star. With power, speed, and strategy, she started winning at a very young age. Williams's time on the court ended when she retired from tennis in 2022. With a case full of medals and trophies, many consider her the greatest of all time (G.O.A.T.).

Read on to find out more about these amazing athletes. Who's the better tennis player? Let the smackdown begin!

Gauff leaps into action during a 2022 US Open match.

CHAPTER 1

Coco grew up in Atlanta, Georgia.

ALL IN THE FAMILY

Coco was born in Delray Beach, Florida, on March 13, 2004. Her family moved to Atlanta, Georgia, when she was young. Her mom homeschooled Coco and her two younger brothers.

Both of Coco's parents were college athletes. Her dad was on the Georgia State University basketball team. Her mom competed in track-and-field events at Florida State University.

Growing up, Coco was a natural athlete. She was a gymnast and played soccer and tennis. She decided to focus on tennis when she was eight. By watching the matches of Serena Williams and her sister Venus, Coco saw that Black people belonged in the sport. She told her parents she wanted to be the best in the world.

Coco (center) with her parents after the final round of the 2017 US Open girls' final.

CONSIDER THIS

Coco Gauff's real first name is Cori. She was named after her dad, Corey Gauff. To avoid confusion, the family started calling her Coco. The nickname was suggested by her aunt. She got the idea because Coco's dad was called Co when he was young.

Coco was accepted into a tennis academy in Florida when she was eight. Her family moved there to support her. When she was 10, she started training at an academy in France. There she learned from the same tennis coach who worked with Serena Williams. Coco was also coached by her dad.

Coco practices in 2023 with her coach from the French academy.

Venus (left) and Serena Williams at a tennis event in 1994

Serena Williams was born in Saginaw, Michigan, on September 26, 1981. She grew up with four older sisters, including Venus, in Compton, California.

Serena's dad started teaching her tennis when she was about three years old. She spent many hours practicing at public courts with Venus. Their dad was a strict coach. When Serena was 10, the family moved to Florida so Serena and Venus could attend a tennis academy.

Richard Williams, father of Venus and Serena Williams, talks to his daughters at a 1999 tournament.

Serena competes in a 1998 tournament.

The entire Williams family took tennis very seriously. But they also believed in education and having fun. Serena did not play in many junior tennis tournaments. Instead, she focused on improving her game without worrying about results and rankings.

CHAPTER 2

Gauff plays during the 2018 Junior Wimbledon Tennis Championships.

ON TOUR

Gauff did well in junior tennis. At 13, she was the youngest person to ever reach the US Open girls' final. She won the junior French Open at 14 and became the number one girls tennis player in the world.

In 2018, Gauff went pro. A year later, the 15-year-old became the youngest player to ever compete at Wimbledon. Her opponent in the first round was 39-year-old Venus Williams. In the first set, Gauff shocked everyone by beating the five-time Wimbledon champion 6–4.

The score was tied four games to four in the second set. Williams looked determined to win as she stepped up for the first serve of the ninth game. She hit the ball hard. The two players hit the ball back and forth five times. Then Gauff won the point by smashing the ball deep into the corner where Williams couldn't return it.

Gauff competes against Venus Williams at Wimbledon on July 1, 2019.

Gauff (right) and Venus Williams shake hands after Gauff wins the 2019 Wimbledon match.

Gauff won that game and the next. She took the second set 6–4. Gauff burst into tears. She'd won a match against one of her idols. The two players shook hands at the net. Serena Williams applauded them both from the stands.

Serena Williams went pro in 1995 at 14. She had several winning streaks over the next four years. A big moment came at her second US Open in 1999.

CONSIDER THIS

Serena Williams has always been interested in fashion, beauty, and design. While playing tennis, she went to college at the Art Institute of Fort Lauderdale in Florida. She has launched both a clothing and jewelry line. Her designs are meant to empower people to look and feel their best.

She entered the tournament ranked as the seventh-best player. She beat the fourth-ranked player. Then she beat the defending champion. In the final match, she faced the number one female player in the world, 18-year-old Martina Hingis.

Serena Williams plays during the 1998 Australian Open.

Williams beat Hingis in the first set. It looked certain that Williams would win the second set as well when she went ahead of Hingis 5–3. But Hingis wasn't going to make it easy for her. Hingis won the next three games and took the lead 6–5.

Williams returns a shot to Martina Hingis at the 1999 US Open women's final.

Williams (right) holds her 1999 US Open trophy beside runner-up Hingis.

In tennis, you must win by two games. So when Williams won the next game to make it 6–6, the set went into a tiebreaker. Tiebreakers are a race to seven points. The players exchanged points back and forth. They were tied at 4–4. Then Williams went on a three-point streak to win the match and the championship!

Her mouth dropped open as she put a hand over her heart. Williams didn't have much time to relax and enjoy the moment, though. With her doubles partner Venus, she won the US Open doubles championship the next day.

CHAPTER 3

Gauff aims for the ball during the women's singles final of the 2023 US Open.

GRAND SLAMS

Gauff's biggest moment happened at the US Open. In 2023, she entered the tournament ranked sixth. She won six matches to make it to the final.

The number two ranked player, Aryna Sabalenka, beat Gauff easily in the first set. But Gauff wasn't about to give up. Her second set win sent the match to a third set. The winner of that set would be the champion.

Gauff led 5–2 in the third set. In the eighth game, she served up rocket after rocket. Gauff won four points in a row to claim the title.

Gauff dropped onto the court, overcome with emotion. She was the third American teenager to win the US Open and the first to do it since Serena Williams did in 1999.

Gauff talks to a reporter after defeating Aryna Sabalenka on September 9, 2023.

CONSIDER THIS

Gauff and Williams are both active on and off the court. Williams's award-winning series, *Being Serena*, and book *On the Line* have inspired people around the world. Gauff uses her platform on social media to speak up against injustice and encourage other young people to do the same.

Over her 27-year tennis career, Williams won 23 Grand Slam singles tournaments. In 2002, she won the French Open, Wimbledon, and the US Open. When she won the Australian Open in 2003, she hit another milestone. She'd completed a career Grand Slam by winning all four of the major tournaments.

Williams holds the 2003 Australian Open trophy after defeating her sister Venus during the women's final.

In 2012, Williams won her fifth Wimbledon singles title. A month later, she competed in the Olympic Games. She won a gold medal in

Williams with her 2012 singles Olympic gold medal

the women's singles event. Having won all four Grand Slam tournaments and Olympic gold, Williams had achieved a Golden Slam.

At those same Olympic Games, Williams won her third gold medal in doubles with Venus. Williams is the only player in tennis history to have a Golden Slam in both singles and doubles. Together, Serena and Venus won 14 women's doubles Grand Slam titles. They have never lost in the finals of a Grand Slam tournament.

CHAPTER 4

Gauff serves during the 2024 Australian Open.

AND THE WINNER IS

Who is the winner of this all-star smackdown? Different people may have different opinions. Both Gauff and Williams are tennis stars. Many people have compared them, but Gauff and Williams never competed against each other on the court.

Gauff has been the youngest player to be the finalist or winner of several tournaments. As a pro, she's won seven Women's Tennis Association (WTA) singles titles, including the US Open. She also won the 2024 French Open women's doubles title with her partner, Katerina Siniakova.

Ranked as the third-best female tennis player in the world, Gauff was named to *Time* magazine's Women of the Year list in 2024. One of Gauff's goals is to win an Olympic medal. Fans can't wait to see her compete at the 2024 Olympic Games in Paris, France.

Gauff poses with the 2023 US Open trophy.

Williams played her last pro tennis match in the third round of the US Open in 2022. Over 27 years on the WTA tour, Williams won 73 singles titles. Of those titles, 23 were Grand Slams. She also holds the WTA record for the longest time ranked as the number one female player in the world. She held the rank for 186 weeks in a row from February 2013 to September 2016. In all, she spent 319 weeks at the number one spot.

Williams hits the ball during her final pro tennis match on September 2, 2022.

Since the moment she stepped on the court, Williams broke boundaries and set records. Very few athletes have won as much as Williams. In retirement, she continues to inspire the next generation of Black athletes.

As the reigning G.O.A.T., Williams wins this smackdown. But Gauff still has a long career ahead of her. Could she be the next tennis G.O.A.T.?

Williams serves during an August 2020 tournament.

SMACKDOWN BREAKDOWN

COCO GAUFF

Date of birth: March 13, 2004
Height: 5 feet 9 (1.8 m)
WTA singles titles: 7
Grand Slam singles titles: 1
Olympic gold medals: 0

Stats are accurate through May 2024.

SERENA WILLIAMS

Date of birth: September 26, 1981
Height: 5 feet 9 (1.8 m)
WTA singles titles: 73
Grand Slam singles titles: 23
Olympic gold medals: 4

GLOSSARY

doubles: a tennis match with two players on each side

game: a part of a set that is won when a player wins at least four points

Grand Slam: one of the four major tournaments in pro tennis (Australian Open, French Open, US Open, and Wimbledon), or winning all four tournaments

homeschool: to teach school subjects to one's children at home

junior tennis: matches where players are 18 and under

match: a tennis contest. A WTA match usually has three sets.

pro: short for *professional*, taking part in an activity to make money

serve: to hit the ball to begin play

set: in tennis, a group of six or more games

singles: a tennis match with one player on each side

Women's Tennis Association (WTA): the group that organizes women's professional tennis

LEARN MORE

Ahrens, Niki. *Serena Williams: Tennis Superstar.* Minneapolis: Lerner Publications, 2022.

Hansen, Grace. *Coco Gauff: Major Tennis Champion*. Edina, MN: Abdo Kids, 2024.

Kiddle: Serena Williams Facts for Kids
https://kids.kiddle.co/Serena_Williams

Kids Reporter Q&A: Coco Gauff
https://www.sikids.com/kid-reporter/kid-reporter-q-a-coco-gauff

London, Martha. *Legends of Women's Tennis*. Mendota Heights, MN: Press Box Books, 2021.

Sports Illustrated Kids—Tennis
https://www.sikids.com/tennis

INDEX

PHOTO ACKNOWLEDGMENTS

Image credits: AP Photo/Michele Eve Sandberg/Icon Sportswire, pp. 4, 28; AP Photo/Shuhei Yokoyama/The Yomiuri Shimbun, p. 5; AP Photo/Andy Wong, p. 6; AP Photo/Corinne Dubreuil/Abaca/Sipa USA, p. 7; joe daniel price/Getty Images, p. 8; AP Photo/Corinne Dubreuil/Sipa USA, p. 9; AP Photo/CHRISTOPHE SAIDI/SIPA, p. 10; AP Photo/NewsBase, p. 11; AP Photo/Al Messerschmidt Archive, pp. 12–13; Frank Molter/Alamy, p. 14; AP Photo/Tim Ireland, pp. 15–16; AP Photo/Rick Rycroft, p. 17; AP Photo/Kathy Willens, p. 18; AP Photo/Roberto Borea, p. 19; AP Photo/John Minchillo, pp. 20, 25–26; AP Photo/Frank Franklin II, pp. 21, 27; AP Photo/Steve Holland, p. 22; AP Photo/Rebecca Naden/PA Wire, p. 23; AP Photo/Alessandra Tarantino, p. 24; AP Photo/Kyodo, p. 29.

Cover: AP Photo/Rebecca Naden/PA Wire; AP Photo/Mark J. Terrill.